TAKE A SPADE AND A BRUSH LET'S START DIGGING FOR FOSSILS!

PALEONTOLOGY BOOKS FOR KIDS
CHILDREN'S EARTH SCIENCES BOOKS

BABY PROFESSOR
EDUCATION KIDS

Speedy Publishing LLC

40 E. Main St. #1156

Newark, DE 19711

www.speedypublishing.com

Copyright 2017

It would be cool to dig into the Earth and find a dinosaur fossil! Let's find out what fossils are, and where we would find them.

PALEONTOLOGY LOOKS INTO THE PAST

Scientists who study the history of life on Earth are paleontologists ("paleo" is from the Greek word for "ancient"). To find out about creatures who lived on Earth before humans, they often study fossils. The fossils can tell us what animals were shaped like, what they ate, and a little bit about how they lived. They can sometimes tell us about what trees and insects were like millions of years ago, too.

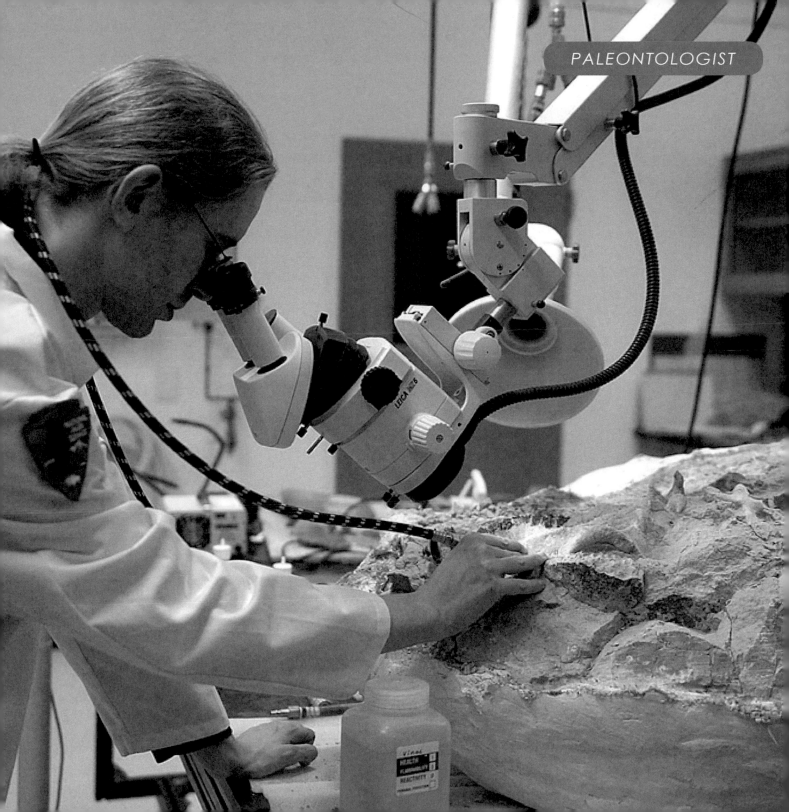

DRY RIVER BED, CANADA

If you go fossil-hunting, you are participating in an exciting effort to find out how life was on this Earth before we were around to take part in it.

WHAT YOU FIND

What we mainly look for when we study the distant past is fossils. "Fossil" comes from the Latin word that means "it was dug up". We use it to refer to material from plants and animals that died millions of years ago. Fragments of their bodies, or their shapes, were preserved in rock and are just waiting for us to find them.

ANCIENT SHELL STONE

FOSSIL

HOW FOSSILS ARE MADE

When most creatures die, their bodies wear away and disappear. Other creatures or insects eat the soft parts, and acids in the soil, and the flow of water, break down the bones over time. But sometimes things went a little differently!

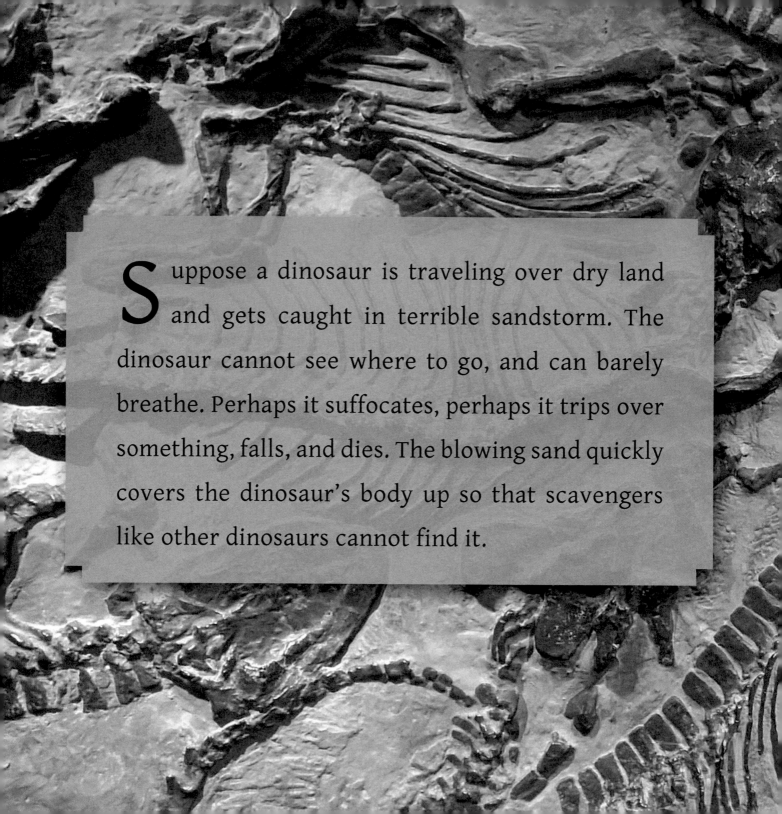

Suppose a dinosaur is traveling over dry land and gets caught in terrible sandstorm. The dinosaur cannot see where to go, and can barely breathe. Perhaps it suffocates, perhaps it trips over something, falls, and dies. The blowing sand quickly covers the dinosaur's body up so that scavengers like other dinosaurs cannot find it.

Slowly, below the layer of sand, the soft tissues of the dinosaur rot away. At the same time more sand and soil is slowly building up above the body. As the layers get deeper, the weight of the sedimentary material starts to compress it together into sedimentary rock, like shale.

PRESERVED SKELETON OF A DINOSAUR DISCOVERED IN CHINA

PRESERVED SKELETON OF A DINOSAUR

While this is happening, chemicals from the material around the body seep into the bones, eating away the original material and replacing it with a rock-like substance. This substance is harder and heavier than the original bone, but it keeps the shape of the bone. Finally, after thousands of years, there is a rock-like copy, a fossil, of some or most of the bones of the dinosaur.

WHAT YOU FIND

Here are the things a paleontologist may find:

Dinosaur bones

Almost all the time, the flesh, skin, and organs of an ancient creature are no longer there for us to find. What we can find are bones, though! Usually you find a few teeth, part of a large leg bone, or maybe part of a skull. It is very rare to find a complete skeleton. More often, a paleontologist finds some teeth in one part of the world, and has to compare them with teeth and jaw fragments found in other places to learn if the new find is part of a dinosaur we already know about, or is part of some creature new to us.

Dinosaur Eggs

Dinosaurs, like modern birds (who are descended from them), laid eggs. The new dinosaurs would hatch out of the eggs. We don't know whether some dinosaur species hung around to take care of the eggs and then their babies until they were able to take care of themselves, or if they just buried the eggs and left them.

DINOSAUR EGGS FROM CHINA

Footprints

Dinosaurs, and other prehistoric creatures, left footprints in mud or clay as they walked through it. If that material had a chance to dry before the footprint was washed away, the footprint may have been preserved for us to find. The footprints can tell us a bit about the creature that made them: how long was its stride? Was it running? Did it have claws on the feet it walked on?

Dinosaur poop

If you have a pet dog or cat, you know how much they poop every day. Now think of a dinosaur as big as a city bus! They created a lot of poop! Most of the poop was absorbed into the ground, enriching the soil, but some became buried in layers of mud or soil and then fossilized.

FOSSILIZED DINOSAUR POOP

Studying dinosaur poop tells us a lot about what the animal's diet was like, and sometimes a bit about their digestive systems.

The photograph b
slice from a copr
dinosaur "poop"
we can figure ou
from a plant-ea
during the Jura
observe the ce
of the undiges

x6

Coprolite sl
Karen Chin

a magnified
silized
e evidence
e coprolite is
osaur that lived
od. You can
ure from some
nt material.

Coprolite →

x50

y of Colorado at Boulder

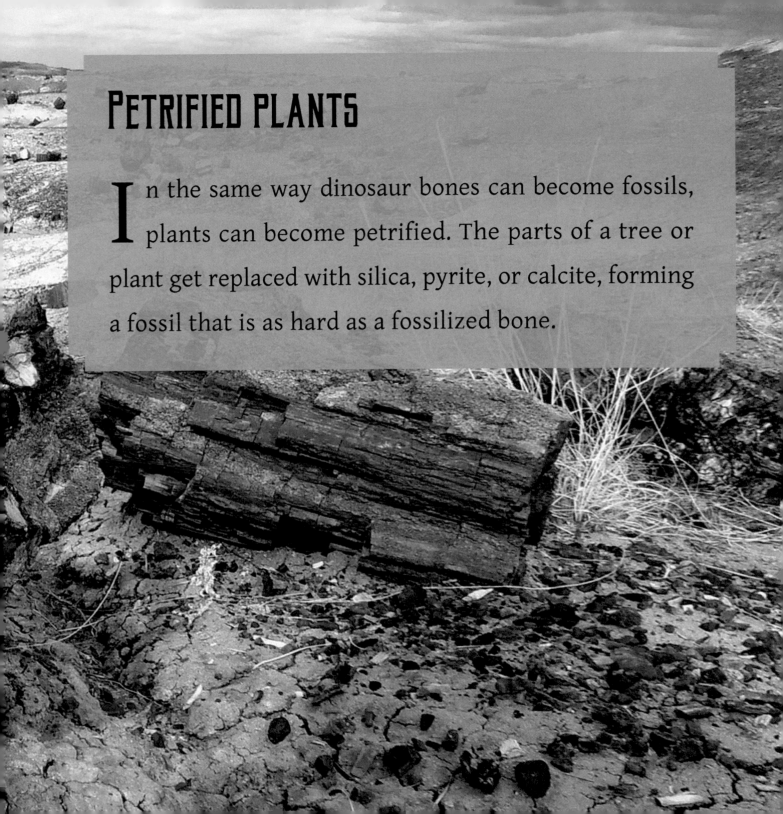

Petrified Plants

In the same way dinosaur bones can become fossils, plants can become petrified. The parts of a tree or plant get replaced with silica, pyrite, or calcite, forming a fossil that is as hard as a fossilized bone.

Trilobites

Trilobites were very common in the Earth's oceans for over three hundred million years, ending before the time of the dinosaurs. They were sort of like insects or lobsters, with tough outer skeletons, legs with joints, and multiple eyes. Many trilobites were fossilized the same way the later dinosaurs were, and when we find one we can look past the dinosaurs into the way life on Earth was six hundred million years ago.

AN ANT INSIDE BALTIC AMBER

Creatures in amber

Many plants, like pine trees, generate a sticky sap or resin. Fossilized tree resin can turn into a honey-colored substance that is hard like a rock and glows like a jewel. Rarely, an insect or even a small animal became trapped in the resin and died, and when the resin became amber the creature was preserved in it. The insects sometimes look almost as they did when alive, right down to their wings and eyes! Feathers of dinosaurs have also been preserved in this way. This helps us understand how creatures looked and functioned millions of years before humans evolved.

THE BEST PLACES TO LOOK

Often the best places to look for fossils are the worst places to live in. Environments that are very dry, like deserts, keep plant matter from sending down roots that could break down and destroy animal remains.

STRATA AT THE FOSSIL BEDS OF PAINTED HILLS

LAYERS OF SEDIMENTARY ROCK IN MAKHTESH RAMO

The next important feature is sedimentary rock. This is rock that was made up of layer after layer of tiny fragments of sand, mud, small bits of rock, and even bone. Heat and pressure pressed the fragments into layers of rock, and in those layers there could be the fossilized bones of an ancient creature.

I t's important to find rock formations of the right age. The age of the dinosaurs stretches from over 200 million years ago until about 65 million years ago. In the United States, a layer of sedimentary rock called the Morrison Formation holds many dinosaur fossils. This formation lies across many of the western states and extends into Canada.

MORRISON FORMATION COLORADO

If you can get there, an area northwest of Beijing, China has been yielding amazing fossil finds in recent years. They include the first proof that there were feathered dinosaurs!

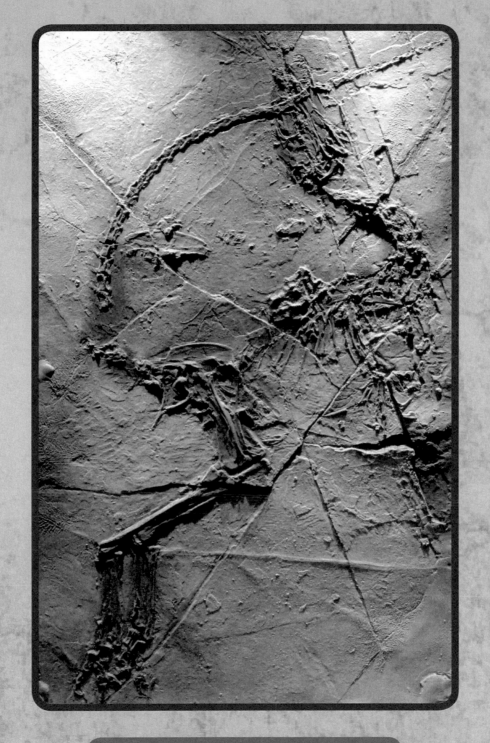

FEATHERED DINOSAUR FOSSIL

What does a fossil hunter use?

O nce you have found a likely spot, with the right sort of rocks of the right age, you need to go to work with the right tools.

The tools fall into three categories:

FOSSIL HUNTERS

Getting the Fossil

Your job will be to free the fossil from the rock in which it lies, without hurting the fossil. For this, you usually can't use power tools. It is mainly a slow, patient job involving hand tools:

- **Rock pick:** this is the favorite tool for rockhounds and paleontologists. It has a square end like a hammer for breaking rocks or pounding chisels and stakes, and a pointed end for digging and for turning rocks.

In a lot of areas there may be dangerous creatures like snakes or scorpions under rocks, so it is better to turn them with a tool instead of with your hand.

Hammers and chisels: paleontologists have as many of these as a painter has paint brushes!

TROWEL

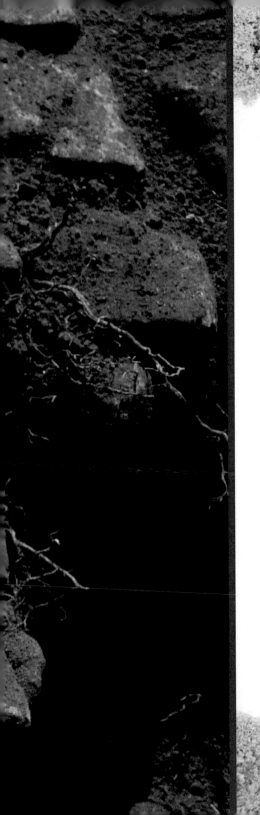

- **Small picks**: you use these to work the fossil free. They can be as small as the sort of tools dentists use on your teeth.

- **Tweezers**: you can pick up important fragments with tweezers without having to pick up a lot of the ground as well.

- **Trowels and dust brushes**: you use these a lot to move dust, dirt, and rock fragments out of your way.

PRESERVING THE FOSSIL

You need some sort of container to put the fossil in. If the fossil is large and delicate, you might have to build a "cast" for it using plaster of Paris and bandages.

EMBRYONIC MAIASAURA CAST

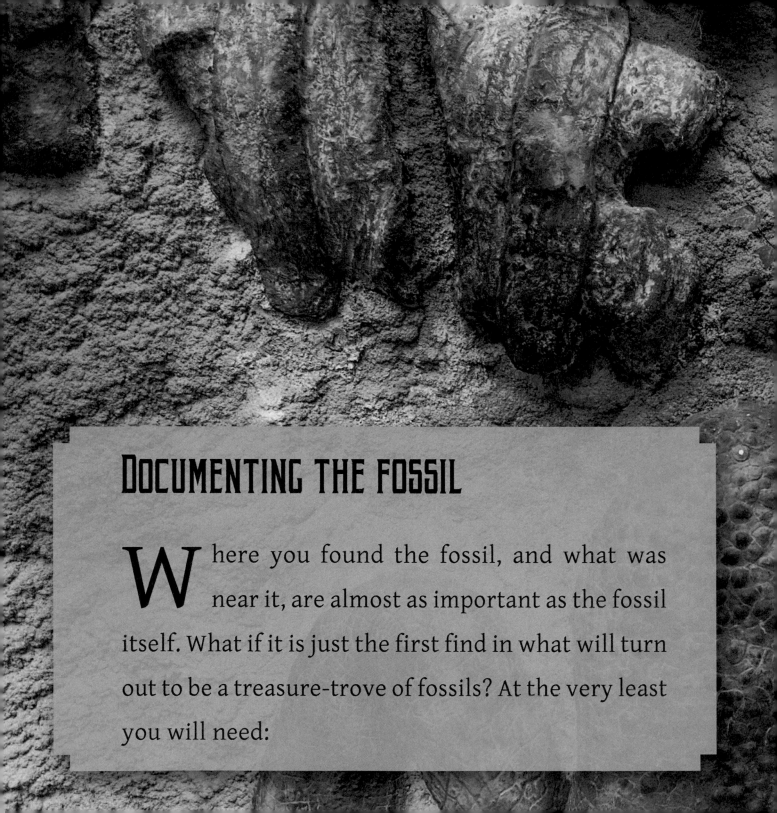

Documenting the fossil

Where you found the fossil, and what was near it, are almost as important as the fossil itself. What if it is just the first find in what will turn out to be a treasure-trove of fossils? At the very least you will need:

- A map of the area, with a compass or ideally a working GPS system on your cell phone.

- A camera, so you can take pictures of the fossil at various stages as you extract it from the ground.

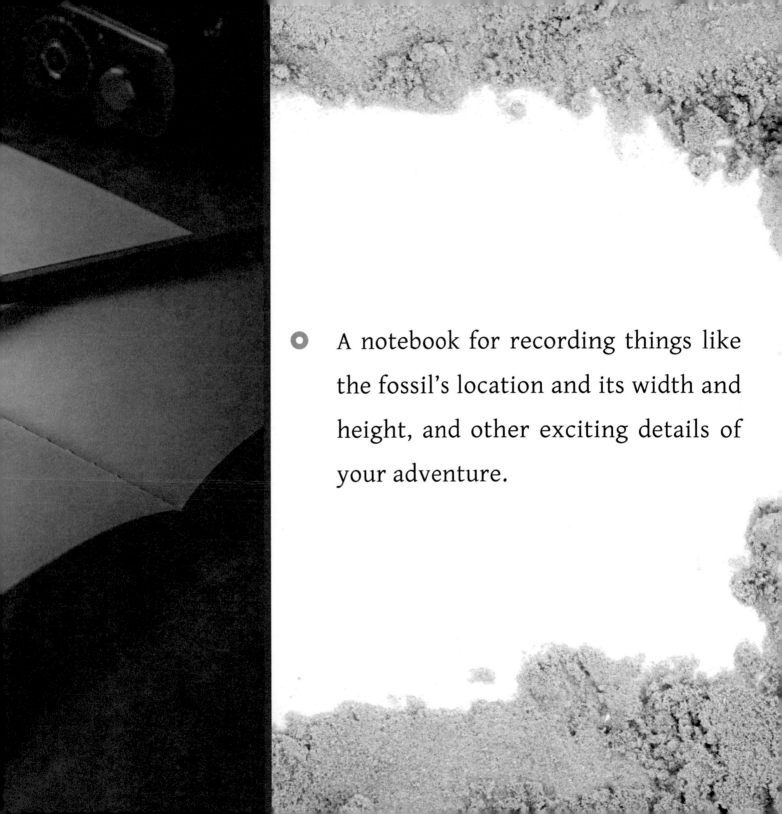

A notebook for recording things like the fossil's location and its width and height, and other exciting details of your adventure.

THE WORLD OF DINOSAURS

What were dinosaurs like? How did they live? Learn more in Baby Professor books like *From Mild to Wild: Dinosaurs for Kids* and *The Big Dinopedia for Small Learners.*

Visit

BABY PROFESSOR
EDUCATION KIDS

www.BabyProfessorBooks.com

to download Free Baby Professor eBooks
and view our catalog of new and exciting
Children's Books

Made in the USA
San Bernardino, CA
19 September 2018